BONO

THE GOOD GUY
WHO ALWAYS COMES OUT ON TOP

RAVE BOOKS

"The name's Bondom, Dames Bondom –

licensed to thrill."

MI7 HEADQUARTERS

Bondom arrived at Mmmm's office.

"Hello, Honeyfanny," he said.

"Double-oh-Heaven, at last," sighed Miss Honeyfanny, fondly.

"Mmmm wants you to go straight in."

"I always do," said Bondom.

MMMM'S OFFICE

"Morning Mmmm. Has something come up?"
asked Bondom.

"Operation Interpussy. You start in Jamaica,
Code name G-Spot – you've been there before."

"In the erogenous zone," Bondom agreed.

"Mmmm," said Mmmm. "Expect plenty of action.
Keep in touch. I want to know your every move."

"I'll let you know the score," said Bondom.

PHEW'S WORKSHOP

"Have you got the right equipment for the job?" asked Phew.

"It's never failed me yet," said Bondom.

He began poking about.

"Pay attention, Bondom. You need the proper kit and an exact fit," said Phew.

"You have to be well prepared in the Amazon. It's a jungle out there."

"I always am," said Bondom.

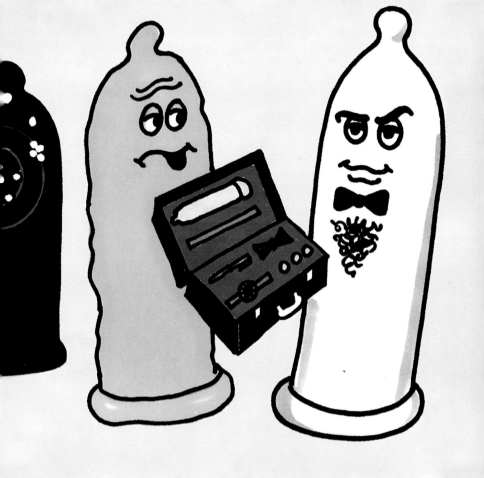

THE CARIBBEAN ISLAND OF DR. OH NO!

The surf exploded as Bondom was torpedoed
from a nuclear submarine on to the beach.

"Who are you?" asked a beautiful blonde.

"Bondom, on Her Majesty's Sensual Service,"
he replied.

"Then I've got something you've been waiting for,"
she said.

"We'll soon see if that's true," said Bondom,
as he started pumping her for information.

ARIZONA: WETFELT'S HIDDEN FACILITY

The ground opened up.

Bondom was plunged into a pool of hungry sharks.

"Goodbye, Bondom, I hope you don't mind being eaten," laughed Wetfelt.

But Bondom whipped out his secret weapon and fended off the frenzied attack.

"I'm not in the mood for a love bite, ladies," he said as he slipped safely away.

ON A PRIVATE JET

Bondom sat down next to the provocative pilot.

"I'm here to relieve you," he said. "Would you like a hand?"

"No thanks, I can manage solo," she replied. "I'm Pussy, Pussy Somemore – and I know what I'm doing in the cockpit."

She pushed down hard on the responsive column.

The jet went into a death dive. Bondom's buckle jammed. Pussy bailed out – leaving him to touch down on his own.

"I knew I could pull it off," said Bondom.

THE STRONG ROOM OF FORT COX

"Give up, Bondom. You won't beat me,"
said S.P.A.N.K.A.

"Don't feel so sure," said Bondom.

The wall by Bondom's head suddenly disintegrated.
Knob-Job's razor-sharp bowler had sliced into it.

"That was a close shave," said Bondom.

He tossed the lethal hat into a generator.

Knob-Job was electrocuted trying to retrieve it.

"I see you still employ bright sparks," said Bondom.

A SKI SLOPE IN THE ALPS

Bullets shot past his head.

"Someone wants me fired," said Bondom taking evasive action.

He gripped his pole as he gathered speed.

"Time I got on top of things," said Bondom.

A SECRET MOUNTAIN RENDEZVOUS

"I hear you got a frosty reception this morning,
Oh-Oh Heaven, so I thought you could do
with a warm-up," lisped the luscious brunette.

"I'm glad you could fit me in," said Bondom.

He was de-briefing Miss Givalott,
his undercover contact.

"There's more to take in than I expected,"
she exclaimed.

"Then let me give it to you straight," said Bondom.

A CONDOMINIUM IN CANADA

Bondom checked into his room. A golden girl lay motionless on his bed.

"Never say live and let lie," muttered Bondom. "Who did this to you?"

"Boldfinger," she whispered as she gasped her last.

"I thought I recognised his handiwork," said Bondom.

ON A SLEEPER, SOMEWHERE IN EUROPE

"The train's so full, we'll have to double up,"
said Bondom entering the cabin.

"I'm sure it won't cramp your style, darling," said
a soft female voice. "I poured you a glass of
champagne, and I need refilling."

"I'll drink to that," said Bondom and he slipped into
action.

"You're just so good at giving a girl what she wants,"
sighed the voice.

"Nobody does it better," said Bondom.

INDIAN OCEAN: HARDO'S YACHT

Bondom sneaked aboard the yacht
to release the trussed-up redhead.

"Quick, quick, we've got to get moving,"
pleaded Triple Sex.

"Then grab hold of me," yelled Bondom,
and he shot off like a rocket.

A huge explosion ripped the yacht apart.

"There's nothing like a good bang
when you're not expecting it," said Bondom.

THE ESCAPE POD

Bobbing in a gentle swell, Bondom was relaxing below.

"How do you like it, Bondom?" asked Triple Sex.

"Shaken, not stirred," he replied.

The satellite phone buzzed.

"Bondom… it's Honeyfanny. I've got Mmmm for you."

Mmmm spoke. "Splendid work Bondom. Well done. You must be very satisfied. What are you up to now?"

"Bondom… Bondom?… Are you there, Bondom?..."

"Just coming…Mmmm…Just coming…"